May the remainder of your days be glitter free (or at least glitter-lite)

Jess Bruder

THE GLUE FAMINE

The Glue Famine

by Lee Bradford
Copyright © Lee Bradford and
Cannibal Coalition
thecannibalcoalition.com

Cover design and
Interior illustration
by Lee Bradford

About the Author
Lee Bradford was once quit their job as kitchen head by way of haiku:
> Its not worth the time
> To officially resign
> I'm burned out; I quit.

And so began a very... interesting work history.

If anyone tells you that retail work is 'easy' work for people who don't have any useful skills, then it is probably safe to say that they've never actually been on the other side of the counter. I say this as someone who has had several jobs of varying difficulties. Craft retail, specifically, sits somewhere in the middle of all these experiences- having its own good moments and bad moments.

But if nothing else, crafting is something that I know a lot about- which makes me a valuable member of the team. And this is why, I suppose, the horrors of the past year have been diverted specifically to me.

This, and the Fates know when a person is a storyteller and opt to provide them with a wealth of material.

It was December 18th, 2016 when we noticed that all the glue was gone and we had no clue why. It was the holiday season, so we were a little preoccupied with the chaos that comes with being in this particular business at this particular time. So when the cavernous shelf was filled, only to be emptied again immediately, we began to speculate.

After all- it was the holidays. People perch themselves like vultures on the strangest items as soon as Halloween is over. Red pony beads, table-top Christmas trees, clear plastic ornaments, paper filler, cookie tins- just to name a few.

Something as simple as Elmer's Glue, although a little oddball, did not seem an unlikely victim for whatever might have been caught in the crosshairs of a Pinterest trend. The same thing had happened not six months ago with string gel medium, which the average crafter has no knowledge of, because a Pin-board suggested it for a tutorial on artistically aging photographs.

We'd survive- whatever it was.

But that was before we started getting the phone calls: "Do you have any glue?" "Do you have any styrofoam pellets?" "Do you have any borax?"

The moment the word 'borax' was mentioned, I knew immediately what was affecting our glue supply. It is a common science project for kids to make glue slime, which is done by mixing borax (a household cleaner) with school glue until it makes a gelatinous semi-solid. This is a great way to teach kids about chemistry and some basic physics. And the wonders of science or... something.

So at this point, I had come to two conclusions, both of which were false: either there were a lot of kids doing this for their science fair project or a lot of children learned how to make it and were showing off to their friends.

In either situation, I was in no way prepared for the reality.

The phone calls became more frequent, urgent:
"Glue?"
"Clear glue?"
"Borax?"
"Shaving cream, contact lens solution, glue?"
"Glue glue glue?"
"Where is the glue?"

"Why don't you have any glue?"

"WHY DOESN'T ANYONE HAVE ANY GLUE?!"

I did what I always do when unreasonable quantities of singular items have suddenly reached an apex of ridiculous popularity: I asked the Internet. An article landed in my lap (literally, because my only computer is a laptop) about how glue slime has become popular. Thousands of videos of people playing with slime. At least a hundred tutorials and recipes.

The other part was about how kids who make it were selling it. There was an entire market in the 7-17 demographics bracket based around the buy, sell, and trade of non-newtonian fluids by the ounce.

And just like any other *thing* that happens in this town, the parents had gone completely bonkers that their children jumped on the trend a day late and started blaming us- because it was entirely our fault that this trend blindsided everyone.

People began showing us just how little they know about working in retail by asking why we 'don't just order more glue?' They felt that it was an affront, a personal insult to them, that we were refusing to do this specifically because of their requests and we are clearly anarchists bent on dismantling this oppressive system.

I had no way of knowing that this was so widespread. I thought it was just our area that was out of glue, but apparently it was the entire United States.

Now, the children approached this trend with youthful abandon. Generally, they were a little sad that we don't have any glue but choose to instead raid our glitter and vow to search for glue elsewhere.

However, the parents know what power is. They pretend to think we have it.

Every day. 9am, on the dot:

"What do you MEAN you don't have any glue!? ITS A BASIC CRAFT ITEM! YOU HAVE TO HAVE GLUE!"

"You're telling me that you DON'T CARRY GLUE?"

"I'm calling your corporate office to tell them just how wholly unprepared you all are because this is the fourth store I've called and NONE of you have any glue."

"Can I pre-order? What do you MEAN I have to order from the website?"

"When will you be getting more? You don't KNOW! HOW CAN YOU NOT KNOW!? Two weeks at the EARLIEST!?"

"Can you call me when you get some? YOU CAN'T EVEN CALL ME WHEN YOU GET IT IN?"

I once caught one of our framers taking a call like these and I saw her re-inact Winona Ryder's entire range of facial expressions a la 2017 SAG awards, eventually ending in her left eye going slightly wall when the angry parent finally hung up.

And there were some that called every single day, asking the same questions and hoping that they'll get a different answer.

But no. I'm sorry. The Glue Fairy didn't make a surprise visit last night. We did not plant the glue seeds in time for the harvest and now there is a glue famine. The small child that we sent to fetch more glue has been captured by witches- who are now intent on raising her as their own and we wish them luck.

One day, my brother will have children and they will ask me about the Glue Famine of 2017 and I will recall a very specific instance wherein I could feel flecks of spittle coming through the end of the phone.

One day I shall die and a team of necromancers

will raise me from my crumbling sarcophagus and the very first words from my revived husk of a maw will be 'WE ARE STILL OUT OF GLUE, CRETINOUS FILTH!'

Every time we'd get some in, it'd get snatched right back up again because desperation means that its every man for himself! I'd suggest bulk orders, but people seem woefully unaware of what that even is.

People think that buying ten mason jars is a bulk order. People think that buying the same package of red pony beads from a retailer and begging for coupons to abuse is better than buying from a wholesaler. People think that spending all day in one store so that you can abuse said coupons over and over again is the same as wholesaling. People seem to think that we, a retail store, are a wholesaler.

Humans have absolutely no concept of what things are actually worth. Monetary value isn't really a concrete concept.

But I digress- ah yes: the glue.

We wagered that this fad would fizzle out with the return of the sun, but oh- we were so wrong.

I cannot begin to explain just how wrong we were.

And that is why this story is so long.

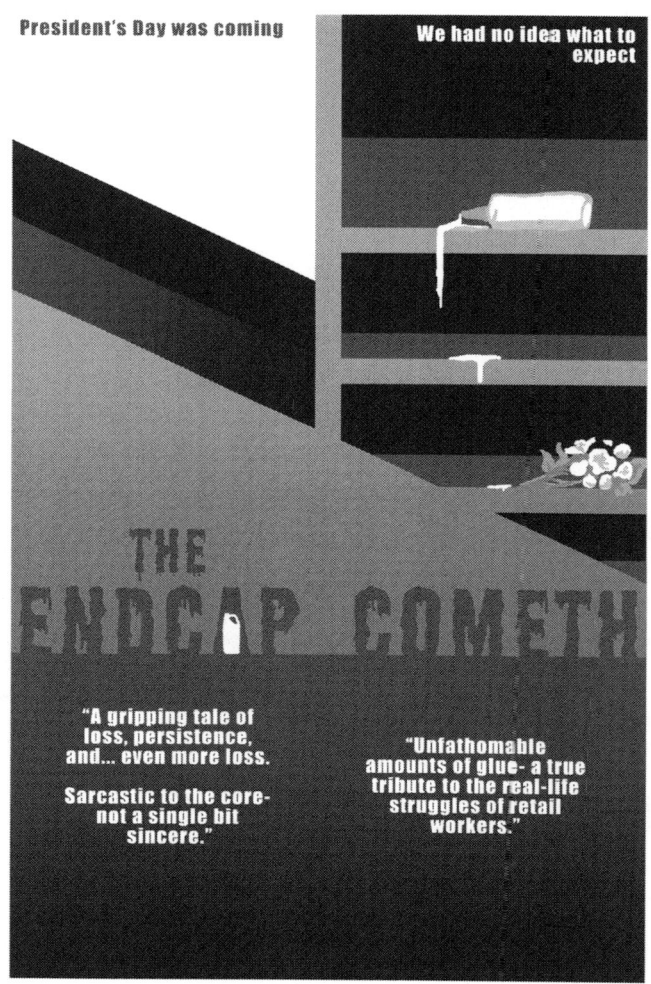

I began documenting the Glue Famine around late January when we had gone a solid month without being able to keep up with the demand. Our resident cynic assured us that they would forget all about this in two weeks before they went back to being distracted by their phones. Because 'those dang young whipper-snappers and their mo-bile telephones don't know what it was like back in my day- we had to walk sixteen miles in the snow, uphill both ways, to get to our internet connections.'

Sure, Brad. I'm like three years older than you but... sure, Brad..

I believe it was also late January when I learned that we were going to be setting up an endcap specifically to peddle slime-related wares: glitter, food coloring, paint... glue. Of course, the glue would be there. Glue is the main component of this trend. Why would we ever leave out glue?

You know why.

It should be noted that for the past two months the glue was completely absent. We would get it in, of course, but someone let slip the secret of when our shipments arrive and soccer moms across the suburb would be right at our door every Wednesday, 9 in the morning, to take it from us because their child's glue endeavors were so much more important than anyone else's and, arguably, anything else that might be going on in their lives.

So, as you might imagine, the endcap would remain quite empty as well. The great big blue and green signs that hovered on all sides of this display were liars. The object of your desires is outside your sticky grasp. Gaze upon my shelves of glue and see that they are barren.

You have to imagine the position we were in here- where we were advertising glue that does not exist for more than three days every two to four weeks because of these tots are hell-bent on selling slime to their sandbox buddies.

We're not selling glue. We're selling the concept of glue. We are selling the desire for glue. We are inspiring others to covet the glue we do not have. The glue is unknowable. It is invisible, intangible, ineffable. One day the glue uprising shall be upon us, and none shall speak its name.

For about two weeks during this time, people were insistent on finding alternatives for glue. The demand for glue was so high that people were asking us for glue recipes and I honestly didn't know how to tell people what glue is made of.

Desperate times called for desperate measures, none of which worked. Flour and water didn't yield good results. Melting glue sticks culminated in a mess. Attempting to obtain glue from cans of spray adhesives... I honestly should not be surprised that someone actually tried to cut open an aerosol can. I should also not be surprised that the grown adult who told me this was sporting a brand new eyepatch.

Because the dozen or so rows where we used

to stock our glue were now a gaping cavity of woe, our heathen customers had decided that this was the perfect space to lazily put things that they just suddenly decide they don't want anymore. And for some ridiculous reason, the most popular thing to leave where an associate can find it... was fake flowers.

People were attempting to build a memorial to the glue that was, and will never be again. The time of glue has passed, we shall remember it fondly. Ashes to ashes, goop to goop. In Elmer's name we pray- amen.

I'd had several people contact me about an email that went out from our company, advertising Glue Slime and giving out a recipe (instead of borax, using baking soda and contact lens solution... I wept for our local optometrists). Luckily, we were sent a large ration of glue on Thursday in preparation for the endcap that we just put up.

And for a moment, the balance was restored. We could rebuild! There was enough glue to fill the dozen or so places in its home and have a good amount for the display. Sadly, we were only given a few bottles of clear glue- which is the one that people really want for hashtag aesthetic reasons. But things were looking better!

But little did we know...

... President's Day was coming.

And the children... needed something to do.

By Monday morning, they had ravaged our glue surplus to 1/10th. The glue that filled its home space was completely gone. I was honestly surprised that the meager 40 bottles we had left were still there and by the end of my evening shift that day, they were not.

Why would you do this to us, Mr President? This was not mentioned at all during your campaign trail and I demand answers!

So while we had those 40 bottles, we could at least fend off the screaming parents, but a considerable amount of screaming had already started by the time I arrived for my evening shift.

I shall scream as well.

I scream, they scream- we all scream into the yawning void of the glue section in hopes that the Elmer, God of Cheap Adhesives, will hear our cries and grant us the glue we so desperately yearn for. We shall be united in our despair.

By March we had reached a place in our glue stock where we were consistently keeping up with demand, more or less. We'd get it in on Wednesday, they'd all come in on the weekend and we were out by Monday- giving people one day to bitch and moan because what would these people do if they weren't allowed to scream at us for a whole thirty seconds?

On one such Wednesday, I was greeted at the customer service desk by a one-gallon bottle of glue annotated with a post-it:

"We Now Have the One-Gallon Bottle of Glue- It's on EC 83; =D" By Fallout Boy.

There were 20 of them on that endcap. I saw a woman buy three of them at once (and of course she wanted to use a coupon on each and every one of them because 'gosh- who knew that glue would be so expensive!' Like… lady- you're getting this at 20 cents an ounce if you get it without a coupon. That's pretty damn cheap and like… we gotta ration this shit for the masses.)

By the end of Wednesday, they were all gone. We sold 20 gallons of glue in four hours. People were laying down $60 for it. I could feel my Great Depression-raised grandpa shaking his head from…. I dunno, probably Purgatory.

Now the entire area knew that we had the glue gallons- the word had spread. But we didn't have them in stock and guess what emotions they had over it!

If you guessed 'anger' then you're right! So they do what they've always done when they need a literal gallon of glue and there are no gallons of glue to be had: they buy a ton of individual bottles.

But now knowing that there is an easier way to do this that is yet inaccessible to them fills them with ennui, and as they walk through the store their excitement over their hoard wanes and they put some of it back.

Now, any person of the retail-worker persuasion will tell you that a customer never puts an item back where they're supposed to. That would be, frankly, preposterous. So instead, as they lose their grip on their desire for glue, they leave a single bottle where it is most convenient to them- a symbol of their defeat.

The short version: I found a bottle of glue in every aisle one night because someone got pissy about not being able to buy it by the gallon and forgot to get a basket.

Eventually, the phone calls slowed down to a reasonable and manageable level. People only called if they needed to know whether or not we have the gallons and believe me: they were not pleased when they hear the answer 'we carry them but are currently out of them.'

Not. Pleased.

Purchasing smaller bottles was not an option, even if it was the only option less than a month ago. The smiley face hastily drawn on the gallon bottle of glue taunted me- a vision of forced pleasantry for the truly, truly exhausted. After awhile all the complaints sound like goats bleating and I imagine that I am peacefully roaming the countryside.

I became unfazed when the bleats became shouts. Boisterous yelling had become the rhythmic breath of the store- rising each weekend and falling to inhale by Monday.

In mid-March, I was promoted to the shipping operations specialist, which is a fancy way of saying that I stand in the back and frustrate myself with uncooperative cardboard boxes.

The Slime Endcap was likewise promoted to what we call a Drive Aisle- which is a simple way of describing 'that thing on wheels in the middle of the aisle with all the seasonal junk on it.' And with it, thankfully, was a shipment of enough glue to repair Indiana's crumbling infrastructure. It was, of course, gone within the first week, but our shipments came in increasing number until our aisles were toppling over with a surplus of glues in frightening variety. Elmer, god of cheap adhesives, had forgiven us of our trespasses and blessed us with a bountiful harvest. The Glue Fairy now makes weekly visits.

The small child we sent to fetch more glue still lives with the witches. They are doing well.

We still played this tug-of-war between supply and demand for weeks and weeks until we finally started getting enough in per week to keep all the shelves full. Not just white and clear glue, but all assortments of glitter glues and compounds. Even a type of glue formulated specifically for the making of the slime! (I have never seen anyone buy this.)

We had reached an equilibrium. I could see an end to the madness.

Oh, but this was not the end. And the madness was only beginning.

We will start this chapter with something of a flashback.

In June of 2016, I was working on a weekend when a man came up to me and said that there was a mess in the men's room. Now, I am no stranger to human waste due to the wide variety of terrible jobs I have worked in the past and I thought 'how bad could it be?'

This is generally a story for a different time, but I will say that there is a Golden Corral across the parking lot from my store and the moral of the story here is that you should chew your food thoroughly before swallowing. Especially if your food is five pounds of pulled pork and roasted shallots.

A manager came in to see what was taking me so long and exclaimed:

"Oh my God- it's chunky!"

The happy ending is that, to thank me for spending over two hours cleaning the walls of the men's room, this manager bought me an egg McMuffin.

Hot tip: Retail people are easily bribed with food.

This is foreshadowing, which means that we'll get to it in a minute.

I thought that, given the impersonal nature of my title change, I would be safe from the chaos of the sales floor and by extension the slime fad. However, as a means to squeeze as much labor out of me as humanly possible, the People In Charge have seen to it that I will be the person to teach the weekly classes. This is generally uneventful, given that no one ever came to the evening classes and the kids classes were sparsely-attended and at least I was given the good grace of having a chair to sit in for a few hours.

As I walk through the valley of the shadow of death, I take the monthly event calendar with me as reading material.

I flipped to the final page and what do I see?

EASTER SLIME EVENT

No Easter basket is complete without spring's hottest trend: Slime! Customize your slime with glitter, confetti, googly eyes, and more!

Now, if you have spent any time in our stores, you will have read that in *Her* voice. Who is *She?*

She is the disembodied voice that separates each fifteen minute block of ironically upbeat songs- about leaving your day job to follow your dreams and go fishing- to inform you cheerfully of whatever is arriving at our store this month. I often imagine a Kind Folk-ish giggle after each ad as though The Unseelie Queen Herself is dictating her itinerary. There is no giggle, of course. It is all in my mind- or is it?

One specific ad which I remember vividly was informing us of all the glitter spray paints available to the masses, because it wouldn't be Christmas without glitter, now would it?

The possibilities and the glitter are endless.
Endless.
Endless...

But back to the looming slime event. Which one of us has been consigned to lead this class?

Oh, you know…

Fate has funny ideas about a person's place in life. I may be given promotions and I may be given pay raises and I may be sequestered into the cardboard fortress of solitude that is the shipping center, but I will never, no not ever, escape the constant sticky messes that craft retail have to offer. At least this time it wasn't a biological hazard.

But here's the kicker:

Because we don't sell baking soda, borax, shaving cream, or contact lens solution, we technically can't have the kids make the slime themselves.

We have to make it and then bring it in for them to customize as they please.

Our manager left in the middle of the day to get supplies to do a test run because she has never made glue slime before and wants to test the recipe that the Company gave us. She came back to the break room as I was coming back from lunch.

Over the headset, I heard: "Oh my god, it's sticky!"

I find an amusing sort of symmetry in the fact that this was the same manager whose response to the aforementioned biological hazard was "oh my god, it's chunky!"

This is that 'foreshadowing' thing I mentioned earlier. You'll learn that there's a lot of that in this story, at least for a non-fiction piece.

The days leading up to this event filled everyone

involved with it with dread and meticulous preparation. An entire gallon of slime had been made prior to the event and portioned into Easter eggs to ration each child's daily allotment of slime. Little cups of glitter, beads, sequins, plastic animals, googly eyes, and (enigmatically) pom poms had been filled and set onto a table covered in paper for easy cleanup.

We had been chanting to ourselves: "It's only two hours, it's only two hours, it's only two hours." This has become the heartbeat, a mantra between raucous breaths of angry parents.

We have played out every possible scenario that could happen and built a contingency plan around every problem. Our armor is on. We have backup.

We are ready for battle.

And now, submitted for your approval, I bring you to April 8th.

Which is, by some weird coincidence and because the Fates like a good laugh, also my girlfriend's birthday.

The managers were more nervous than anyone about this because the Company will be watching our numbers for this endeavor. They want to know just how many people attend this class so they can measure it up against our glue sales and act accordingly. I was pressured to make a good impression- to make this an event that will go down in history.

History is written by the victors and there are no heroes here.

For a bunch of people intent on locking themselves into the office for the entirety of the two hours, they certainly made a fuss about it. I was told to smile many times.

There was another class that I had to teach before I did the SLIME BAR and it was just some silly little Easter craft object of little significance. I got to the end of the class and I started having dangerous thoughts.

What if no one shows up?

This does not come from nowhere. In the sixty classes that I'd been asked to teach since my title change, I'd had people attend a grand total of ten. There were at least five easter egg hunts in the area, several pre-Easter celebrations, and some kind of… soccer thing that were all happening at the same time as the SLIME BAR.

Maybe no one will show up.

As the word 'up' died away in mental echoes, a woman popped her head into my classroom.

"Is this the slime thing?"

I severely underestimated the siren call of the slime bar.

"This is where we're having it, but it doesn't start until 1."

She grumbled and disappeared.

I returned from lunch at 12:30 and there was already a line forming at the door of the classroom.

"Is this the slime thing?" It's not the same woman as before, but a near-identical woman with the exact same poultry-esque haircut.

"It doesn't start until one, ma'am."

She folded her arms at her chest. "I can wait," she said in a tone that indicated that no she certainly will not wait.

I quickly began setting out the individually-portioned cups of glitter and other inclusions, the slime-filled eggs, the parchment paper. I heard a murmur outside, getting louder and louder and louder… more agitated.

The door opened and a co-worker shuffled in.

"There's a line of like… twenty people out there," she said. The room is built to house, at most, twelve. The table takes up most of the space and there is just about enough room on either side of the table for one-and-a-half people to use as a walkway.

"Please tell me you're here to help."

"I have been… encouraged to help."

"Extra hours?"

"Extra hours."

This is the language that we speak in retail. Two extra hours on your paycheck is the difference between an overdrawn bank account and making rent for the month sometimes. She works two jobs. She is already exhausted, but aren't we all? Two hours when you're already this tired is the point that you throw your hands up and proclaim 'why not' before downing an entire pot of coffee.

As an aside- I do not recommend drinking an entire pot of coffee. This is a terrible way to find out that coffee is a laxative.

It became one-o-clock and they all filed in. All twenty four, plus their parents, standing around the table because they apparently didn't understand me when I said 'come in, have a seat.' I called a framer to get us some extra chairs. He brought exactly one.

Thanks, Andrew. So helpful.

Immediately, a little girl started crying because she was under the impression that we were going to have them make the slime instead of customizing it and this has thrown a wrench in her entire day. She was not the only one who was upset over this development because apparently all anyone ever saw in the flier was 'MAKE' and 'SLIME' and all the other parts were decidedly unimportant details. Eight of the kids are upset, three are crying. Oh good- they're learning disappointment early. I have become receptive to the cries of children. I am immune.

Each of the kids were given an egg and they began smooshing whatever particulate they could find into brightly-colored semi-solids and the crying uplifts to joyous discovery as they learn all the ridiculous things they can do with slime. Despite all the various things we have provided for them, they only want to work with glitter. They really were at a loss as to why we would want to use pom poms. No one really knows why they were a suggested item.

A tiny human poured the entire contents of a bowl of glitter into her hand and looked me square in the eye.

"What would happen," she pondered aloud, knowing full well that I would protest the very suggestion. "If I..." She mimed the action of throwing glitter in the air.

"I would prefer it if you didn't."

Of course, if you tell a small human that you'd prefer if they not do a thing it generally results in the doing said thing. Tiny fistfuls of sparkly particulate went shooting into the windless air, arching artfully over the table before scattering into everyone's personal space. Everyone's projects were now magenta. People were mad.

She knew full well what would happen. I could see it in her shit-eating grin full of tiny, perfectly square teeth.

I predicted this. I saw the future and the words 'glitter' and 'sticky' came up in my crystal ball. Mind you, I'm getting paid just above minimum wage here- so the crystal ball is more like... an overturned fishbowl. You can imagine how effective that is.

It is amazing how many things can happen in the course of an hour. This was put into perspective when I looked at my watch. It had been twelve minutes.

Time is relative.

As the first wave of families began to take their oozing babies away to hopefully cleaner activities, a man came in with his twelve-year-old daughter.

"We'll have you sign in," I told him. "Name and phone number in case of an emergency." The girl joined the rest of the glitter monsters while I spoke with her dad.

"This thing ends at 3:00, right?"

"We are holding the event until 3, but the activity itself takes about fifteen minutes."

"I'll come back in an hour just to be sure."

"It's only fifteen minutes."

"Yeah, an hour."

He turned around and left.

The girl was done in less than fifteen minutes and began asking where her dad was. "I'm sure he's in the store." I was not sure. I was super-duper not sure. I had a rotating cast of slime children to attend to and keeping tabs on a fully-grown adult was outside my pay grade.

The girl did not seem impressed or convinced in the slightest by this answer. At the half-hour mark, she got tired of waiting for him and my co-worker escorted her out into the store to see if he was anywhere. Nowhere to be found. 45 minutes, still missing. They call him.

Now, there is a sign prominently displayed in the room saying that we are happy to keep an eye on any children left in our care, but we kindly ask that any parents or guardians stay on the premises in case of emergency. It is also printed on our brochures, on the sign-up sheet, and I even made a little welcome sign that says not to leave children unattended.

It should be known that while I don't hate kids, there is a very good reason for me not wanting to have them and it is the same reason that I don't like being put in charge of other people's children for extended lengths of time. That reason is responsibility. I can't trust myself to make sound decisions in regards to the future of humanity.

Don't leave your children with me! I'll teach them naughty things like self-love and how to question authority! And they'll come home with a sense of self-worth and… and… they'll grow up to dismantle oppressive systems. Trust me! Just trust me! You do not want me in charge of your children, I will teach them how to unionize.

A woman once offered to give me her newborn baby with complete seriousness and I promptly threw up in the trash can at my feet at the very idea of being in charge of a small human for any amount of time. So being left with a small child, a precocious one, whose father is mysteriously missing and appears to have no intention of coming back- is my worst nightmare.

Where the fuck is he?

At home with his feet up. He finally arrived at 2:15 to get her and if that went on any longer, I was going to call Child Protective Services because holy shit, you just dropped your kid off in the care of complete strangers juggling two dozen children at any given time.

According to the girl, he always does this. Including one time where he made her wait three hours to pick her up from school because he was watching television.

I don't make it a habit of judging a person's child-rearing techniques because I don't intend on having them myself but HOLY FUCKING SHITBALLS.
WHY?
WHY?
But that part of the nightmare is over.

It was now 2:30 and the influx of children had slowed to a trickle. The initial urgency to do the 'slime thing' had waned and there were at this moment only a few people in the room. We could breathe. We were suddenly aware that the room smells like glue fumes and that we'd been inhaling these the entire time.

I did a final count on the roster. Fifty-two.

Fifty-two. Four dozen excited slime children have come and gone in two hours. This is a lot of things to happen in a short amount of time. But it is almost over now. It's almost done.

A small child toddled up to me and handed me an egg.

"I made this for you because I love you."

It was at this point that I realized that the eggs all had holes in the bottom.

And that was the last of them.

There were four messages on my phone, all from my girlfriend asking me when I was supposed to be out of work, that her parents were here and that they were all going to dinner. My lunch consisted of a cereal bar that I found in my purse.

So I cleaned up as fast as I possibly could, wiped down everything, swept, threw out the rejected slime experiments, put things away, scanned the used items out of our inventory and I was out of the classroom as fast as I could be.

But on my way back to the break room to clock out, the one-chair framer caught my attention and had a customer ask me: "How do you make glue slime?"

My cells are vibrating with urgency and anger. JUST. GOOGLE. IT. Just fucking google it. You have all the information in the world available to you in the form of an overheated black rectangle in the palm of your hand.

"Glue. Water. Borax." These are the ingredients chosen to create the perfect little mess.

Flying out the door because my girlfriend is urgently asking where I am. They're tired of waiting for me and want to move on.

I arrived at the pizza parlor thirty minutes late and covered in a fine layer of glitter. There was a googly eye stuck to my butt.

Her parents know me well enough to know that this is not unusual. They somewhat expect an amount of glitter to come pouring out of my pockets when I meet them straight from work.

Listen- I know what the obvious joke here is. 'Glitter is the herpes of the craft section.' Not only is this a rude, often-repeated joke, it is also entirely wrong. Herpes symptoms are often undetectable. Glitter, on the other hand, is immediately detectable by everyone but yourself

I managed to somehow maintain a perfectly shimmery topcoat on my lips for the duration of dessert. Now, this seems like it might be the culmination of all the awfulness wrought from the Slime Fad. I would love to tell you that the rest of this book is filled with photographs of the stray cats living behind our dumpster. But believe me when I say this: this is just all just rising action. There are more horrors to come.

It had been an entire week since the incident and the stock of glue had risen and fallen in odd intervals as people bought glue, then returned glue that they didn't use, and then bought the glue that they actually needed, only to return it again. If the shouts of angry parents are the breaths and our ongoing chants are the heartbeat, then the uneven quantities of glue on our shelves are the slightly distressed gurgling of something resisting digestion.

On Monday morning, the drive aisle was completely empty of glue. At least three times a day, I had people asking me when we would get more.

Now, it has been my experience that it is an awful idea to reveal to your customers when your truck comes because that means that we will have people camping out at exactly ten-til-nine in the morning to be the first to get whatever item is of their utmost desires (in this case- glue.) We also never know what is on the truck until the truck gets here, so there is no guarantee that the highly-coveted glue will be on that truck. It is best not to get their hopes up.

Well, someone let it slip that our truck generally shows up around Wednesday. When I find out who it was, there is a curse waiting for them and you can bet it will involve glue.

I came in on Wednesday morning and… all the replenishers had gone home.

Oh no. I knew what was happening before I asked, but I opened my mouth to speak.

As though sensing my troubles, the manager informed me:

"The truck is somewhere by the side of the road. We don't know when it will get here."

One woman, who somewhat resembled Melissa McCarthy, claimed that she had been waiting WEEKS for a gallon of glue and that if she didn't have something with which to make slime so that the kids could keep themselves busy during what was looking to be a rainy Easter Sunday, then her entire plans were

RUINED.

I wondered if Alec Baldwin was waiting slightly off-screen.

The drive aisle remained an empty tomb.

Throughout the week, people kept asking about our 'slime-filled eggs.' "They would make GREAT basket-stuffers! Where are they?"

"… we don't sell them."

"But you're advertising them!"

"They were part of an event on Saturday. We had kids make them."

"You… don't have any left?"

"We can show you a recipe to-"

They turned.

They left.

They walked straight out the door, into the parking lot. As the automatic doors began to close, I heard the rising pitch of a frustrated scream. Several of the resident geese were disturbed. It is inadvisable to disturb the geese on any occasion. Offerings of stale bread were made in swift apology.

For those unaware of the presence of geese in the upper American Midwest, it must be known that many shopping strips such as the one that I work in have been built on the remains of a former body of water. Geese have a migration pattern that has them returning to the place of their birth each year and you might assume that upon finding their breeding place to be nothing but a cold slab of concrete they would find a better place to raise their young.

You would be wrong.

Instead, we have a flock of increasing quantity arriving every spring. If you know nothing about Canada geese, you must know: Canadians may very well perform a ritual each year where they pour all of their nastiness, rudeness, and ill-demeanor into a flock of geese and the rest follow suit as they migrate southward.

It is this, or the fact that a family of them roosts right next to our door and people are complete idiots when it comes to interactions with wildlife. Some answers to common questions include:

"Yes, those geese are real."

"No, they are not dead. They are asleep. Do not approach them, they are not sick. They are, however, jerks."

"Yes, I realize that they are harassing customers. I cannot, however, control wild animals. Yet."

"Please do not take selfies with the goose."

"Please do not leave 3-foot high piles of moldy bread for the geese to eat."

So far, no one has actually been bitten, but we have had to put a cart by the door to prevent Daddy Goose from hissing at his own reflection in our windows and leaving a trail of goose poops up and down the sidewalk.

So you must understand- they believe that this is their store. We effectively rent this space from the geese, who so far have been generous (albeit unkind) landlords. The occasional offering of stale bread in apology for the noise disturbance is the least that someone could do to prevent an incident.

But that's geese. This is about glue.

I had resigned to the possibility that we may never get this truck, but the following Saturday I walked in and saw that the entire drive aisle had been filled! The Glue Fairy visited us in the night and granted us our most pressing wish. Elmer, the god of cheap adhesives, had forgiven us for our glue-related sins and blessed us with a bountiful harvest.

And then I learned that our regional manager was set to come in and the place has to be spotless.

This goes double… for the classroom, which had not been cleaned since the SLIME BAR.

Listen, I did the best I could the week before. I put down paper, I wiped down all the surfaces. I swept, I removed sticky items from the chairs.

But as anyone who has ever dealt with large amounts of glitter could easily predict- the entire room was still sparkling like a David Bowie tribute band with a special guest appearance by Kei$ha.

When slime finally dries out, it develops a texture similar to rubber cement- which means that it's still picking up random dust and debris and looks somewhat like boogers. Sparkly boogers.

On every conceivable surface.

Wipe down, dust off, scrape up… doesn't matter- there's still more.

About half an hour into my cleaning spree, a

woman and three children came in.

"Is this the slime thing," she asked.

"I'm sorry, but that was last weekend."

"You mean you aren't doing it every week?" Remember that 'foreshadowing' thing I mentioned? Keep an eye on the little red dot.

"Just last weekend."

"But I told my kids that it was THIS weekend!"

My brain felt like the several seconds in which a bag of microwave popcorn begins to all pop at once. There was a ringing in my ears as I began to think of all the sarcastic responses one might have to this, all of them processing at once- all of them fighting for dominance over my power of speech and yet all I could say without getting immediately fired from my job for reasons of sass was: "I don't know what to tell you."

There are some sounds that only dogs can hear.

This was not one of them.

But I had become accustomed to the screaming. I am immune. I have taken this poison so many times that it no longer affects me. My blood screams. It vibrates at the exact frequency of middle-aged mothers and delights in the cries of disappointed children.

I am an anger sponge. You cannot hurt me.

On April 19th, I took photos of our glue drive aisle because for the first time since we had started this gods-forsaken trend we actually had all of the items that we advertised. I also learned that we were going to have a second slime event on the 29th. This was the start of... many.

It should be no surprise to anyone that I am a fan of Welcome to Night Vale. Anyone who has ever met me will be able to immediately tell. And they were doing a live show on the 29th and I had booked tickets as soon as they became available in February- long before any of this slime nonsense. I requested off and got it approved so that we could treat it like a date. As people who work service jobs, dates are few and far between. Days off are spent either doing housework or trying not to move. Most 'dates' are just... communal naps. So an actual date, where we go places and do things in a public place where we are not in some kind of uniform, is a big deal for us.

My boss complained to me that everyone asked that date off as if they somehow knew that we were going to be having an event. After two and a half years of working here, I had discovered that if she is complaining to you it is because she wants you to fix it.

Begrudgingly, I volunteered as tribute- but under the stipulation that I have the following day off.

"Ah. Going drinking?"

"... I need to sleep at some point, Pam." Pam assumed, in general, that if you were not working then you must be out drinking. Because why would any of us ever have a social life? What even is this 'going out' thing that the youth seem to be doing these days if it doesn't involve a bottle of whiskey? Who are your friends and why don't they work here?

And so, I was scheduled for Return of the Slime Children.

For the next two weeks, we compared notes on the last slime event to make sure that we didn't fall into the same problems as we did last time. We didn't bother with pom poms. We made sure the only pony beads we had out were the glow in the dark ones. We only had some of the googly eyes. We had an abundance of glitters. We only made clear slime. We have added styrofoam beads to our inventory.

We made sure we knew the number for Child Protective Services. I mean... just in case.

Throughout this, the glue drive aisle ebbed and flowed like an ocean of curdling milk. We were nearly out of gallons by Monday, filled again by Wednesday, only to slowly disappear again. If anyone was looking for plastic containers, we deeply apologize- they're gone.

I was less stressed about the event this time than I was last time. I had done this once, I can do it again.

On Saturday morning, I parked my car and prepared to walk through the rain and wind to meet my fate.

Lightning.

And then… **THUNDER!**

The car shook and I could feel the vibration in my chest as the rain poured down harder. My windshield gave me the illusion that I was drifting slowly beneath the surface of a swiftly-moving river. The sky was dark, wind rocked my sedan in measurable increments and the Payless Shoe Source was consistently backlit by a furious electrical storm. A flock of crows taunted me from the streetlamp.

Growing up in Indiana has somewhat warped my sense of storm safety. We once had a family reunion during a tornado and as soon as the wind stopped we went back to eating our corn. We don't even go into our basements anymore when there's a storm warning, we just switch to a TV channel that isn't showing the weather.

So my thoughts on all of this were very dismissive: well, this was certainly ominous.

I have learned to suffer ill omens after years of working in retail. Every day is going to be a bad day. I willfully ignore my impending doom. Every doom is impending. It's what doom does: it impends.

"It's gross out today," one of my co-workers said, as though I had not just walked through an entire deluge. "I don't think we're going to have a lot of people coming."

Oh…

When I was just out of college, one of the many jobs that I took to keep afloat during The Recession was giving out free samples of things at the grocery store. They had us mark on our sheets what the weather was like that day to use as a gauge for future data.

What I learned was that the weather has little to no bearing on the actual attendance of a free event happening indoors. We were open during a blizzard once and people braved the snow and wind to buy crafts for their bored children. The myth persists, however, that the weather correlates with participation.

1pm rolled around, we were prepared. Unlike last time, there was no line at the door and for a moment I almost believed the myth that rain affects attendance. I joked with myself: *maybe they're all trapped in the Bahamas.*

My boss, being ever-so-helpful, decided to make an announcement:

"Attention shoppers: iiiiiiit's SLIME TIME! We are hosting a free slime event today from 1-3 and your kids get to take home their very own slime."

These are words that my boss would never expect to say ever. She was just as confused by the slime trend as anyone. You could hear it in her voice as it echoed across the aisles. Uncertainty wavered in the rafters, hanging in the air like a cloud.

All at once, four teenage girls came in, giggling. "We're here for the slime thing."

We motioned for them to take one of the bags of slime and they just… they tore straight into them and got right to it. They went immediately for the styrofoam beads and just started dumping their slime right into the bucket. The air was crackling with the sound of air pockets popping open.

Previously, I have thought it an unfair stereotype to imply that teenagers of this decade are obsessed with colloquialisms native to Social Media, but their commentary for the nearly thirty minutes that they did this was as follows:

"Hashtag SLAY"
"Hashtag YAAAAAAAS."
"Hashtag Do it for the IG"

Author's note: I really want a fucking hashbrown. Editor's note: every time I've read this, I have also wanted a fucking hashbrown.

After awhile, the 'hashtag' joke started getting a little old and one of them just started saying 'slime slime slime slime.'

The rest of them joined in: "Slime slime slime slime."

The smaller children in the room began to mimic this behavior- to the dismay of the parents. "Slime slime slime slime."

Soon we had an entire room of children in all age groups droning a monotone chant of *slime slime slime slime.*

You cannot stop children from chanting. I have learned this through trial and error. Saying 'please stop' only encourages them to rebel against authority. Which I'm all for, but not when that authority is me.

This went on for about ten minutes. My boss popped her head in to see what the commotion was about and I just put my hands up in defeat while she retreated to the safety of anywhere else. She did this often.

This eventually calmed down. The teenagers left, it was quiet.

While this event is marketed towards little kids, a number of younger children don't really understand that you're supposed to put things in the slime and then moosh it around for a minute. If you're about three years old, all you understand is that there is GLITTER.

One of the things we encourage people to put in their slime is these little soft plastic animals- which come in dinosaur shapes.

A very small child eschewed the slime entirely, grabbed a couple dinosaurs and dumped red glitter straight onto them.

"Oh sweetie, what are you doing?"

"COMET!"

The dinosaurs died because of glitter. This has been decided. I don't see it being an incorrect conclusion, in hindsight. If I were a tiny dinosaur and a gigantic toddler threw sheets of plastic on me I would voluntarily become extinct.

Another child decided that the slime was the backdrop for THE FROZEN TUNDRA and built what she felt was an accurate replica of Elsa's Castle- complete with tiny bison. It was made with silver glitter and beads. She screamed when we told her that she's meant to mix it in. When her father intervened, she screamed:

"You broke it! You broke it!"

She rebuilds. Larger, stronger.

"Honey, we can't take it home like this, it's all loose!"

"I have to make it bigger because you BROKE IT."

Now it was a great big mess and they were ready to leave. "Okay, honey. We can't take all of this home. We have to put some of it back." Of course she threw a fit. She's built this entire empire of glitter and who in their right mind would want to destroy that?

Dad would.

He funneled the glitters not attached to the slime into his hand and put it into a styrofoam cup. This includes the bison.

She was not happy. Listen, child- no one here is really happy.

We added her leavings to what we've dubbed 'the mystery mix-' which is whatever glitter has been left behind.

We reached the final half hour of this event and

so far no parents had abandoned their children with strangers so we were already doing pretty well. We started to make attempts to at least consolidate all of the glitter cups in a way that we can get a head start on cleaning.

That's when two teenagers come in.

"OMG is this still going? Can we make slime with you guys!?"

This began the 'hashtag- hashtag' rhetoric all over again.

At the last ten minutes of the event and they said 'can we make another one?"

Since it looked like we were slowing down mostly with still like twenty slime bags left, we were like 'sure.'

The event is ending. No one else is coming in. These two girls were still enjoying themselves. With two minutes left, we let them have the rest of the slime. They spent an amount of time talking about how slime is banned at their school.

…you don't say…

They combined ALL twenty bags together to make what was at least an entire pound of slime. They combined ALL THE GLITTERS and it looked like a weird, purply mass. They decided to see how far they could stretch it without breaking it and it stretched all across the width of the room.

"What's that," said one of them.

"What," I asked, expecting some horrible thing.

"That weird thing floating in the middle."

I went over to inspect the brownish mass suspended in slime, thinking maybe the glitter clumped or something. If that was the case, then stretching it any further would result in a small explosion of glitter as the air pocket expanded and… well… this is my life now- I might as well roll in the stuff.

It was the bison. The bison somehow made it into someone else's project. That poor dude. This is why they were on the endangered list for so long. Well... that and engineered genocide.

They thanked us, they left. We're finished. The official count is 48. Apparently one of the nearest stores had an attendance of 130 and I'm left wondering how? How do you fit 130 people into that tiny ass room?

HOW!?

During the last event, we did not have the styrofoam beads. Anyone who has ever used styrofoam beads in anything will tell you that given the slightest movement of air they will begin to move of their own volition. This makes them a bitch to sweep up. I swept that room four times and there was still a minor snowfall under the table.

As I was taking the garbage to the compactor, I was made aware of a hole in the garbage bag. This also made me aware of the trail of glitter I was leaving on the floor. Determined not to leave this job to someone else, I threw the bag away and got a dustpan to clean it up.

I swept up most of it into the dustpan and was rising from my crouched position to throw it away when I felt a tap on my shoulder.

Startled, I jumped slightly.

Piff!

An eruption of glitter and dust rained down on me, hitting mostly my scalp. I tried not to breath it in, but even when I thought it was safe to breathe there were still fine particles of glitter inhaled straight into my sinuses.

The small human child that tapped me on the shoulder asked me where the bathroom is. The best I could do was point.

My shift... was over. I left the premises in a haze of sparkling particulate and exhaustion with the promise of doing something fun tonight.

I didn't have the time or energy to really shower, so I just did a quick pat-down with water and vinegar to get it off my skin. I got most of it out, you can't really notice it that much anymore. When I was done changing clothes, I realized that my hair has been in a ponytail this entire time and that I should probably wear it down since we're going out.

All I did was pull out my hair tie and glitter cascaded down across my face, shoulders, dress, and chest.

I am defeated.

I have rationalized that glitter is probably not the weirdest thing to be covered in at a WTNV Live Show.

(Someone get me a fucking hashbrown.)

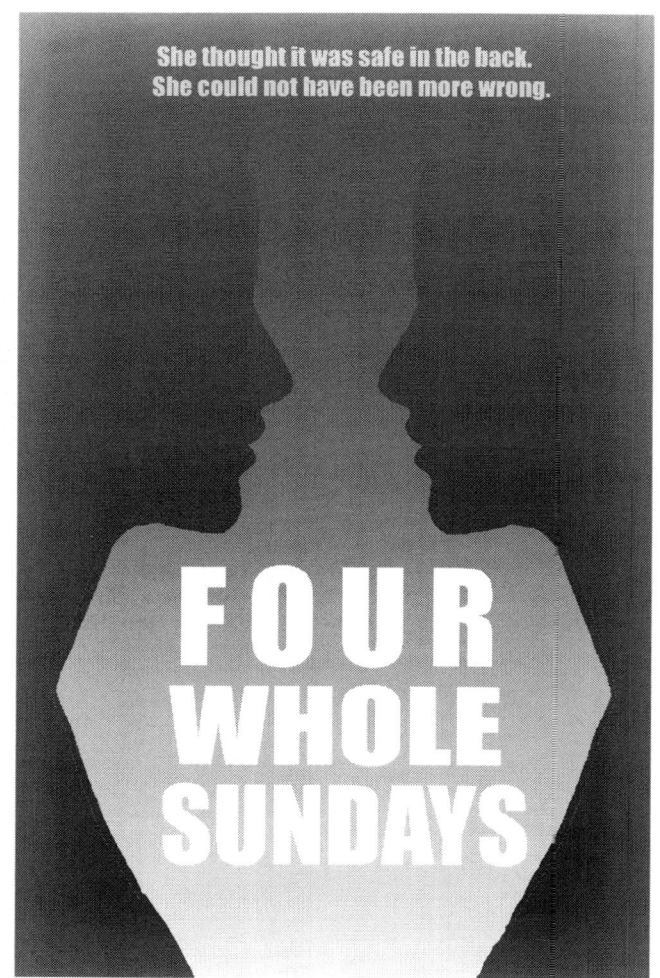

Without much in terms of warning, the Senators of Slime working at our corporate office decreed that June was going to be SLIME MONTH: slime-making events every Sunday in the month of June because we're gonna ride this gravy train as long as it will chug.

I just imagined someone chugging a gallon of glue. Gross.

I had been hiding in the back room for the entirety of this month, so glad that it was decided I should not be made to run the shipping operations AND teach the classes AND run the register AND be the floor expert on most things. Which meant that the Slime Sundays phenomenon skipped straight past me. Of course, this did not spare me from the frequent shouting matches with my boss about not working fast enough, but... hmm... more on that later.

Until the final week, when the dude who was supposed to run it suddenly remembered that it was a cultural holiday for him and opted not to come in- without telling anyone beforehand. Or... anyone knowing that it was a holiday. Retail is like that. Clocks, calendars, and axial tilt are irrelevant. There is only glue.

Which meant that it was down to me to entertain whatever glittery emergency might emerge from the abyss of screaming children.

I was late to work that day because a goose decided to circle my car. Not in the way that a vulture circles, but in the way that a goose does. He waddled slowly around the perimeter of my parking space, occasionally stopping to stare at his reflection in my Ford Focus.

There are few things more menacing than being stared down by a goose who thinks that you're another goose. They come second to turkeys.

I have had experiences with birds. Please believe me- they have been frightening.

I didn't even budge from my spot until he was clear across the parking lot.

In the past month, we had seen a rise in glue-related sales but people didn't really come to the events.

One week prior, we only had about 16 kids show up.

I had mixed feelings about how this was going to go, as I finished up the morning class and assured Mrs. Cleary that yes- the tempura paint is both non-toxic and washable and Little Ashley will not be going to school with purple hands unless she just fucking avoids washing them for two days.

I had learned by now that there are precautions to slime events and there is a limited amount of control that the event runner can have. These sorts of events were not my first foray into the stressful world of event planning. In college, I helped plan weekend events to provide an alternative to binge drinking at my college- which most people would do after binge drinking anyhow, so mixed results. But more recently, I had been put in charge of a birthday party consisting of twenty-eight children, sixteen of which had actually been invited.

No one brought a lighter. We powered through every tantrum. I am the queen of holding it together (at least until the end, where no one can see me crying.) I have dipped my toe into the chaos and begun to find peace.

But there's always that vibrating fear that something unexpected and awful will happen.

I will spoil the surprise- we had something like 32 of them the final week. This is a tolerable number compared to the 52 we had the very first time. I can handle 32.

All 32 of them were disappointed that they were not making the slime themselves (yet again) and I am 100% certain that this is the reason people aren't showing up to these things. They've learned.

Now, these can get repetitive, so I'm going to sum up the day in the manner of a list.

I started the day with an anxiety attack, which was great. My coping method was to rework the lyrics to Disney songs so that they reflect my feelings. "I want to be where the people aren't." "Let me rest, let me rest, let me rest." "I sell glue, I sell it until I want to scream." This carried through the day, even while Pam screamed at me.

-The first wave of children included one who insisted that the BEST things were ones found on the floor and thus decided to incorporate the lovely texture of human hair into their slime ball.

-"What... IS it," asked one of the parents. "No, it's gross!" She said as she continued to play with it.

-A tweenager listed a bunch of instagram handles that feature slime. I promptly forgot them because I was just that interested.

-The bags that we were storing the slime in kept

breaking and our only explanation is that the slime was TOO POWERFUL TO BE CONTAINED.

-One parent just… disappeared. Again. Thankfully, they stayed in the store, but after that first close-call of having to call CPS I was just about to hit the button.

-One helicoptery parent wouldn't let his daughter just play. Like he had to commandeer her slime and show her how to do it the right way and I'm just like… dude… she's like…. two.

-I'm not entirely sure what the demographics are in this area, but at one point I was trying to instruct an entire room of children who only spoke Russian. Hand gestures were useful. Mimicking their accent was not.

-One parent insisted that it was pronounced 'slime-EEEE' and would not back down.

-"Are we going to make edible slime?" "No." "When are we going to make edible slime?" "We're not." "I want to make edible slime." "Too bad."

-What is with little kids and chanting? Did I accidentally join a cult again?

-And then for an entire half hour- SILENCE. No one from 2:15 to 2:45. I was afraid to do anything like cleaning because what if a kid shows up, but no one showed up.

-So I figure- maybe if I stand out there with a ball of slime and play with it, I will attract customers in. I go out there with some goop and start being visible.

-There are no children to be found anywhere in the store. So I'm just standing there, a grown ass adult, playing with slime like some kind of weirdo.

-Suddenly, a group walks in and sees me playing with it and stop in the tracks.

-In hindsight, opening up a conversation with youngsters with "Hey- you kids like slime" is super-extra-creepy. However, that didn't seem to matter because their parents were like 'seems legit' and that's how I got my last group of students.

All of these were very small instances in comparison to the main event- which left me conducting the last half of the show with half of my face covered in white, iridescent glitter. Which I will recount to you now:

A little boy decorated his slime in the same manner that a chef garnishes chicken parm. A little sprinkle here, a little sprinkle there. But he had to carry the entire cup of glitter from one end of the table to his seat to and I noticed that he was holding it at an angle that was certain to tip over and I made a conscious decision to intervene.

"Hey there buddy," I said, getting on his level. "That looks like it's gonna tip-"

'Tip' was apparently the word of the day because as soon as I said it, the entire cup of glitter went tumbling out of his hands, bouncing off a chair and... right into my face.

You are probably imagining this scene happening in slow motion: the cup tipping over and each particle swirling out into the air, spiraling like a cyclone as it heads towards my face, the entire cup of it inverted in mid-air and the contents falling prey to the inevitability that is gravity before being caught up in the air current caused by the only swiftly-moving object in the room until finally upending on my unsuspecting scalp.

None of this happened. The fact of the matter is that one second it was in his hand, and then the next it was cascading down one side of my face like a drag performance of Harvey Dent.

There are people in the world who freak out if a single scintilla of glitter happens upon them. I am not one of them. I have endured a small child's fantasy of throwing magenta glitter into the air, I have soldiered through the dustpan leavings being spattered into my face, I have worked no less than three Christmases at the glittered circle of Hell and I have not backed down.

I once processed a $1029 transaction that was just blue, white, and silver glitter Christmas picks. Pride Festivals would be envious of the amount of glitter that ends up on my skin on a daily basis (and on a side note- I was, in fact, missing Pride for this.)

It was caked on my face and I didn't even flinch. This shit is in my DNA.

One eyebrow had a greater concentration of iridescent glitter than the other. It was in my mouth. An x-ray of my sinuses would blind the technician. It was caked along my forehead and I. Don't. Even. Blink. You. Cannot. Break. Me. I. Am. Already. Broken.

Lee? Why does all this weird shit only seem to happen to you?

Well, disembodied voice from nowhere- statistically, it has to happen somewhere.

But that was the last of them and I was done for the day. I forgot all about the incident with the glitter until I caught my reflection in the rear-view mirror in my car: I looked like I had been given a surprise visit from Carrie Fisher's Force Ghost.

When I came home, my girlfriend had her glasses off and that was the only reason she couldn't see the glitter.

After she'd seen it, she kept edging away from me anytime I got close.

I'm marrying a smart girl.

Are y'all tired of slime? I'm tired of slime. I am so tired of slime.

You know who isn't tired of slime? My employer, who will stop beating this horse when it stops making us money. You know what takes away from that money?

Coupons.

The Slime Senators did not like coupons on their precious glue. And so it was decreed that the gallons of glue would no longer be applicable for coupons. It was listed under one of our special programs with coupon exclusions but oh- no one reads the exclusions.

So it was a common interaction for someone to hand me a coupon for their entire gallon of glue and be met with:

"I'm sorry, but we cannot use coupons on the gallons of glue."

And they would stare at my unmoving face for a time so silent that for a moment even the geese have fallen to a complete hush. I wait. The next move is theirs.

"What do you mean you don't allow coupons on

the glue?"

"It's part of our Value pro-"

"Nowhere. NOWHERE on this coupon does it say you can't use it on glue!"

"We reduced the price so that you don't have to use a coupon to get a good deal on it. The trade off is that we can't accept coupons on them."

"NOWHERE DOES IT SAY THAT."

I kept a highlighter on me at all times for moments like these, knowing exactly where on the coupon the category is listed, then pointing to the sign on the slime display which advertising the exclusion. "There is a sign on the shelf saying that it's part of this program."

"You expect me to READ those signs?"

".... yes."

This is, of course, an example of the average interaction between a cashier and a slime parent. It is at this point that they break their cold stare to frantically search on their phones. "Do you take Retailmenot coupons?"

"Retailmenot copies our coupons, which would have the same exclusions."

"What about Hip2Save?"

"Literally the same situation."

"GROUPON?"

I learned a facial expression from one of our framers. It is called the 'lip curl of hesitant truth.' First you take a deep breath, curl your top lip inward, then your bottom lip, and slowly exhale. This is somewhat less confrontational than the shaking of the head.

However, it is still often met with that kind of throat-scream that parents make when they take things too seriously. It has a somewhat trilling quality to it. Operatic- excellent vibrato. Some of them really can reach those high notes. If only I cared for sopranos.

"Then I. Would like. TO USE. A COMPETITOR COUPON, please."

To which I simply point to sign above my register, which reads: 'Exclusions apply.' Because when I say that we cannot apply coupons to an item- I mean that we cannot apply a coupon to an item. Fight me- I will win.

Lips tight, forming a perfectly circular hole in their face- "Well." Amazing that they can make those sounds while their lips crowded so tightly around their teeth. "I'm just going to go somewhere else," they threaten as they shove the bottle towards me. "I hope you like going out of business."

Oh, I wish. Oh, I desperately wish that it were that easy. I'm still waiting on that robot to replace me and if it doesn't arrive here soon I will start building it myself.

But ah- there's more.

We had an entire month where slime was not even mentioned in our programming. Not a single word through the month of July- it was glorious. I felt like I was on vacation. I mean... not really. Are you kidding me? I work in retail- how the fuck would I know what a vacation feels like?

The slime trend slowed down and I could see the end in sight. The slime display was partitioned to share space with rock painting- which was the hot-new-thing for about two months. (Yes, we did have rock painting events, but oh- they were so much more manageable. You could walk out of there without feeling like you were covered in something.) The aisle that we were carrying all the slime kits was taken over by other science projects and everything was crammed onto that drive aisle. This was a light at the end of the tunnel.

Ah- but of course, that all ended in August,

when Slime was once again a monthly class.

The normal amount of geese to encounter while waiting for my shift to start is generally one. The same father goose, staring into my tail light for an average of fifteen minutes before deciding that I was not also a goose.

But on the day of the Slime's Return, I was visited by quite a lot more. I noticed them approach my car from behind, marching as though to a slow dirge. It began as one, and then another… until my car was completely surrounded by a flock of fifty geese all heading south-east at an impossibly slow gait.

I was engulfed in a sea of waterfowl before they all passed on.

There are not many omens in traditional folklore regarding geese and parking lots, but that certainly was ominous.

But it does not do well to dwell on the meaning of fifty geese when there is slime to be made.

The usual flow of this event begins with a large swath of children in the first half hour, followed by a slow trickle of people in and out, finally tapering off in the last fifteen minutes to a reasonable amount of people.

Classtime began and… no one.

Ten minutes… no one…

Fifteen…

Finally, at the twenty-minute mark, a family of three arrived. They had been waiting for this! They were so excited for the slime! Yeah, me too- sure.

The kids get their slime and…

… have no idea what to do with it.

"You put glitter in it," I told them.

"And then what?"

"You … you play with it?"

I'm at a loss. The kids made me explain to their mother what a meme is. I was informed how to make a fidget spinner out of slime. (Why?) They offered me a one-eyed kitten named Pig. It was really, really tempting.

And that was all for the actually interested parties.

I spent the next hour and a half standing outside the classroom with a ball of slime and demonstrating just how much fun it is like some kind of slime-peddler, shouting 'FREE SLIME' at passersby. Mothers were hiding their children from the weird adult playing with gooey things.

At one point a woman turned her nose up at me and said 'They don't NEED you- they can make slime backwards, blindfolded in their sleep.' Huff huff. Wow. I was unaware that the slime economy had a bourgeoisie. We're about to have a class war with our inferior 'first one's free' slime.

All totaled, we had nine people show up for the class and I had to goad them into coming.
Now don't get me wrong- people were still buying uncomfortable amounts of glue. But there were no further slime events on the calendar, the ads for the slime crafts have slowed down, and we're not pushing it as much anymore.

I know better than to declare this to be the end while there's still a metric ton of glue on the shelves, but a break in the clouds is a break in the clouds and for once… just this once… I came home from work without looking like I swam my way out of a flooded Lush store.

However… whispers seeped into cracks of the concrete bricks and echoed in their hollow caverns. Change was coming, and it would come at us

... quickly.

Forgive me, readers- I have been dishonest.

It has not been a lie so much as it has been an obfuscation of the whole truth. A verbal sleight-of-hand, a herring as red as the evening sun. Of course, this started out being about glue and I agree- this is where our story began and perhaps if I had not gained the support of many who read my tale, I would not have had the confidence to make a very, very important decision.

You see- while the manager, Pam, was thoroughly engrossed in the tick-tick-tick of each dollar in revenue our store gained from glue sales- we linked arms.

I did not discuss this in length because, well, you're not here for stories about abusive bosses- but I hinted. In small ways, I sent out cries for help- and some of you heard me. The details are no one's concern but mine and those of us that conspired, but the whispers began in July and carried us through October. Each time Pam spoke on the headset, we were waiting for another storm, and with each day that passed we awaited a phone call from HR.

When one person makes the call, then that's just one person. And when two persons make the call, then that's two people. Ah- but when seven people: managers, crew members of several years, people of irreplaceable nature... when seven people come together and take it upon themselves to discuss with a complete stranger the shouting matches, the petty grudges, the conflicting orders, and the unacceptable comments of a superior... well I believe that is what you call a Union.

Except you can't say the word 'union' because this is retail.

And it was a tense four months. We wondered with every waking moment when the call was going to be made, if they were going to make a big show of it.

Calls were made over my head and I only heard news as it trickled down to me in tense whispers. Documents were photocopied and passed between workers, signatures were affirmed. And then...

Complete silence. For weeks.

And then, late in October- our District Manager came for a visit.

Now, Pam is no fool. She knew that something was happening. Two weeks prior, someone who had been working for her temporarily was let go during an investigation of forged signatures. And oh- who do you suppose taught her to forge signatures?

So tension swarmed around the woman like a cloud of disturbed gnats. But Pam was an actor- every word she said was dripping with refined, white sugar syrup. You could use her act to make one hell of a pecan pie.

And that day in late October- oh, she knew. Pecan pie for the entire crew.

We didn't know what to expect, honestly. How often does someone orchestrate a bureaucratic mutiny when you're a bunch of novices?

The District Manager came in, sat down in the office, and called her in. He called her in several times, becoming increasingly angry as his patience became thin.

Pam had purposely neglected to put on a headset. His response was to call her over the PA system- like an angry parent embarrassing an errant child.

And in fifteen minutes, she was being escorted from the premises. Passive-aggressive glances to all.

Of course, I'd like to think of this as playing out like the end of an episode of Leverage, where all seven of us stand out in front and gloat while she stomps off to her car, never to darken our door again. But the truth of the matter is that it happened so quickly, so quietly, that she was simply there one minute and gone the next.

And so- our chain of command was upset.

This is related to glue, and I will tell you why in a minute.

Any transference of power will require an adjustment period. There was a stretch of two weeks where our store had no real manager and all our support staff were taking turns trying to pick up the slack. (Although, it was decently fair to say that there was not much slack to pick up. Pam spent a considerable amount of time hiding herself away in the office. I saw little difference.) During this adjustment period, a few things might have fallen through the cracks.

Now, I had been a little hopeful in regards to the slime trend because it looked like it was on decline. The slime drive aisle had been moved away from the front doors, meaning that it no longer took priority. What could possibly take priority over something as culturally important as cheap adhesives?

If you know me at all, then you know that the

answer is Christmas.

It took Christmas, arguably the worst time of the year for us retailers, to force the stacks of glue towards obsolescence.

Truly he is the son of Blob.

Oh, but it's not done. You bet your sticky wiggle eyes that they're gonna ride the gravy train until it derails- killing dozens and injuring hundreds because we know this train ain't arriving safely at the station. TOOT TOOT!

Wanna know why I know that it's not done? Because there were a surprising number of people out there in the world who seem to be under some mistaken notion that we're having slime events every week. Literally- there's always at least one kid that comes into whatever class they have me teaching that day that immediately cries when they find out that slime was last week. And do the parents listen? Haha- nah.

So the Saturday prior to this travesty, I was visited by a mom-and-daughter who wanted to know about the slime class the following day. And I was like- wait hold up. Because we were definitely having one the next Saturday, but there was nothing on the schedule for Sunday. She scrolled through her phone until she found the ad and sure enough- an email went out sometime this week advertising a slime class for Sunday The Fifth. The florist handed me the leader guide and I'm like… great.

It's Christmas-themed oh goody.

Every time we think this trend is dead, someone sticks electrodes into this trend and screams "ITS ALIIIIIIVE!"

Hashtag: theythoughtIwasmadattheuniversity
Hashtag: Iminsaneaboutthebrain
Hashtag: firebad

The schedule wasn't up yet, all I knew was that I was in at 7:30 am on Sunday.

In limbo on this, I was mentally preparing myself for the possibility that there was more glue in my future.

I came in Sunday morning and as we were stuffing the ad, I asked the manager on duty: "What time am I out today?"

"Looks like 12:30."

The slime class starts at 1. SAFE!

Ah. Haha. Oh- haha… you all know what's gonna happen- right? Like by now, you're all so invested in this nonsense that you've figured out the pattern, right?

Like I don't have to explain to you what literary irony is at this point because currently I am a living embodiment of the only verse in that Alanis Morissette song that actually qualifies as 'irony.'

"Follow-up question: Did Elle (the person in charge of classes) make the slime for today?"

"I believe she did."

Remember that bit about foreshadowing like… six months ago?

Anyways, putting up the ad took me to ten-o-clock and I had two and a half hours to get all the orders done- which is pretty doable. I mean on a good day I can get everything done in less than an hour, and on a bad day it takes maybe three.

Except- oh, haha- except: instead of my usual 15 orders, there were 35. Twice plus more of my usual workload and no one warned me. So I didn't take my usual fifteen minute break so I could get the workload done. And I was so close. At 12:03, all I had left was Christmas trees and I can just do them all in a bundle and be done- I have got this.

And then there's Hannah on the headset: "Do

we know who's doing the slime event today?"

Assistant manager, in front of me: "Oh, Lee's doing it."

The hell she is.

"Uh… no. No I am not. I am out of here in half an hour."

"Okay so no she's not."

"Follow-up question," I asked again, because this is a completely different manager than before. "Did Elle make the slime for the class?"

"She's supposed to make the slime?"

"She's made the slime every time we have a slime class. It's the way we've always done it. The event wasn't on the calendar, which is why I'm asking."

"…what?"

"So the answer is no, then."

She tapped her foot, which is something I've noticed she does when she is unsure of what to do next.

"Do you know how to make slime?"

"Yes."

"Can you stay til 2?"

Every bone in my body resisted what I was about to say. I had the entire day planned. I was going to go home and cry off the most stressful week of my life while listening to smooth jazz and procrastinating on an art commission. I was going to eat junk food and yell at the TV. I was, just this once, going to be a completely boring person.

"I can stay til 2." My teeth were grinding against each other. She probably heard my jaw pop.

"Okay.' Tap tap. "I'll have Donna run the event and then you can make the slime in the meantime."

All the materials for slime making were in the classroom: we got our glue, contact lens solution, and we even have this nifty like… thing that Elmer makes specifically for slime making. Hail Elmer!

However... ah- oh... goodness. We only had two of those. One of them makes two batches of slime. And we're out of baking soda.

With twenty minutes left before the show starts, we were out of one of the key ingredients for the main event. As one of our framers rushed out the door to get some, a small family walked in.

"We're here for the slime."

Pause. Check watch. Someone didn't turn their clocks back. "It doesn't start until 1. If you could come back in about fifteen minutes?" I mean, they're not happy but at least they weren't waiting at the door like that one lady always does.

In the meantime, I'm gathering glitter and trying to get things set up with Donna. Fun fact- Donna was the mom that offered me the cat named Pig. She came to the slime show a few months ago and said 'I want in on this.'

She's never made this herself. Neither... really have I- I just know the principle.

Baking soda arrived and we praise the twin demigods Arm and Hammer for this blessing. But it didn't matter. None of this matters because I'd only made four bags of it and it was

.

sLIiEMe. HIimE

Immediately, children arrived as I was furiously trying to figure out ratios. Dry to wet, contact solution to taste (ew). Donna was just about as pleased about this as I was, but we're getting through this. Orders were divvied out in such a short amount of time that I did not get a chance to eat anything and I was not only hangry, but I was HANGEROUS.

Laser-focus on this hocus pocus.

I just get needed to get through this hour and then I could go eat something finally.

The first kids came in without a word. It was absolutely quiet in there except for the rhythmic flop-flop-smack-glorp of me mixing this goop together. They stared intently at the slime as though speaking too loudly would spook it.

This ended when a group of four or five children came in and yelled "SLIIIIIIME!"

I paid attention to nothing but getting this made-to-order slime properly mixed. I have got this down to a science. I hovered over this cauldron of bubbling green concoction on this Slime Sabbat and ignored all other things until I at least had a crate full of this oleaginous curse.

Donna took charge of crowd and glitter control. She is handling it. She is on it. I am on it. We exchange a slime-five.

My hands are now blue.

I've made enough to sustain the kids that were in there and decided that while she's got a handle on the whole deal I might as well stand outside like some kind of slime siren looking for kids to lure into this glittering doom.

Except for some reason, at 1:30 in the afternoon on a Sunday, there are no children to be found- again.

So stood out there- starving, tired, looking a little too intense, and covered in slime. I have become an ornamental hermit.

Finally, my dreams have been realized.

The last group of kids in there left at exactly 2:00.

I went in to give Donna basic instructions on how to do an easy clean-up and how to make sure inventory is done and other crowd-control things. And then I left.

At some point during the day, I managed to develop a limp. Starving, tired, intense, covered in slime, and limping- the ornamental hermit is on the move. And it is chaos outside the classroom. Line is reaching the middle of the building, cashiers were all tied up with complicated transactions, there is no one on the floor to find items or answer questions because everyone is on the register.

And I...

...don't...

Care.

Oh... oh gods, I do not care. I had been here since 7:30, there has not been a single moment where I wasn't busy, I haven't eaten, I'm in pain, and I'm covered in weird green stuff.

I don't give fucks- big or small.

Taco Ding Ding never tasted so fucking good in my LIFE.

Hours later, I was still picking slime bits out of my clothes. So that was nice. My hands were flaky. And still blue.

I wrote the first draft of this while sitting in the waiting room at Urgent Care.

That's a very dramatic opener, so don't get too excited about any stories about socking someone in the mouth because that didn't happen even if I really... really... really wanted to.

Our new manager had been introduced to our crew on a day that I was scheduled off. She had been in and out of the store, always out of my sight, always on opposite schedules- for a good week. But the stars had aligned on Saturday that we would both be opening and finally I would be able to meet Pam's replacement.

Now- the day prior, I was made aware of the fact that our slime event, which was exactly as difficult as putting slime in a clear plastic ornament, was featured on Good Morning America (or something.) And I knew- just knew, that I was going to be the one stuck doing it, even though the schedule had me out before the class started.

None of this was actually surprising because we've been featured on GMA a couple times before and people get weirdly invested in whatever craft item we're putting together for the day.

What was surprising was what happened at approximately 10pm Friday night- when I started falling asleep and all of a sudden my jaw WAS UNABLE TO MOVE.

This was not the first time that this had happened to me.

'Oh Lee! Tell us the story of how you first threw your jaw out of whack!'

Well to make a long story short- I was living on a mountaintop in Montana and had a vivid dream about getting into a brawl at the bar/pizza parlor across the parking lot from my log cabin. I couldn't tell you why I was having this dream or what it meant- all I knew was that everyone was hitting everyone else and someone socked me straight into the face. And I woke up with a jaw that popped and one hell of a neck-ache.

So my life was forever changed by the happenstance of DREAM PUNCHING.

Now, during times of stress, my jaw will occasionally lock itself up and be unable to move. Usually, I deal with this by re-aligning it and just going about my business. But this time it just wouldn't budge. Every time I tried to move it I was met with unforgiving resistance and a sound like popping violin strings in my inner ear.

Now, those of you living outside the United States have probably figured out that we Americans have a complicated relationship with healthcare. There was no way in hell I was going to the hospital. I was not going to be able to afford the visit. So I stood there in the bathroom, whimpering, and trying to knock it back into place while my girlfriend tried to find an Urgent Care place that's open at 10pm. Surprise- there is none.

And just as she was about to make a for real emergency call- I popped that sucker back into place like the badass that I am.

Needless to say- I did not get much sleep after that.

So I figured that I was just going to lay low for the day and try to get as much work done as I could without talking to anyone. I held my jaw kind of funny to prevent it from seizing up again and I could talk without pain but I didn't want to stress it too much and I would just go to the UC after work. My teeth hovered apart from each other by about one half of an inch and it took tremendous energy not to bite my tongue on every breath.

So upon first meeting, the new manager had the impression that I am constantly holding a small bird in my mouth.

I got back to my desk and there was a note asking me to take care of the kid's morning class and the Slime event in the afternoon. Because I'm the only one who knows how to run one properly.

The... complicated relationship with healthcare also applies here. Because I gotta be able to pay for the doctor's visit. Which would cost about a day's pay and... well... hours are hours. And now I've got a small bird to feed.

Insert criticisms of capitalism here.

The morning class also involved large amounts of glitter and it was ridiculously well attended. If you advertise glitter to small children, they will come in droves with the explicit purpose of making a giant mess. I didn't have time to properly clean up. My technique for dealing with this is to tape paper down on every individual table and then a long strip of paper covering the entire surface so that I can just roll all the remnant glitter in one go.

It's genius, but I mean no one is safe from the glitter. NO ONE.

When I finally got a break, there was glitter in my coffee. It's just... it just is. It is what it is, okay?

Glitter in my coffee- whatever. Hashtag aesthetic, I'm sure. There isn't anything you can do about it. I had exactly fifteen minutes to change out the papers and set out the glitters and every other gods-be-damned thing they want us to put into it. I was not about to ruminate over glitter in my coffee. I just fucking drank it. Caffeine was more important.

This too shall pass.

The sales floor was an absolute madhouse, of course- it was one week until Black Friday and everyone was losing their collective shit early. I gathered an armful of glitter containers and on my way to the classroom a woman stopped me.

"Do you have more of these wreaths? I need twenty-six of them."

Why would you ever need- ugh, nevermind. "What we have in that aisle is what we have." As I was beginning to turn and leave-

"There aren't any in there. Can you check the back?"

"If that's the last one in there, then that's the last one."

"But I need TWENTY-SIX! Can't you tell me if they're at another store?"

It is important to note that I was carrying more than twenty containers of glitter and eagerly stepping away from her whenever there was a break in the conversation. They do say that much of our communication is body-language, but I think that it would benefit a number of the population to take a few lessons in 'subtle hints.' I had about five minutes to get into that classroom, and I did not have time to call every store so that this single person could have twenty-six perfectly matching Christmas wreaths for whatever extravagant purpose she might have in mind.

"I'm sorry, I don't have a way to look that up." I turned and ran for the door before she could say another word.

On two hours of sleep with an aching jaw, glitter in my stomach and running entirely on one cup of coffee- I did not have time, energy, or patience to deal with more than one problem at a time. If she made an angry call to the store, then that was the manager's problem.

However, the life-sized Santa Claus figure standing by the door was watching me through the window of the classroom- so I guess I'll be getting coal this year. Maybe the government will start to care about my rights when they find out I could single-handedly revive the coal industry by way of naughtiness.

Just another way that Slime is destroying America, I suppose.

What they didn't go over on Good Morning America was the fact that you and your slime child would be doing this in a room with at least twelve other children. The presence of a dozen delighted children was heralded by their delighted screams and before I could even finish setting out the materials, they had already torn into all of it. I got three minutes into this and the place was already a mess. All the neatly-organized inclusions were contaminated by other glitters, the bucket-o-slime was already depleting, and a small child was following me around for reasons I couldn't decipher.

Everywhere I went, this tiny blonde girl was close behind, as though she wanted something from me.

I hadn't seen her come in, I didn't know which ones were her parents. I was beginning to believe that I was the only one that could see her.

Go.

Shoo!

If I solve a riddle, will you leave?

She did eventually disappear into the rising cloud of glitter and I wondered if perhaps I ought to have said it in Russian, but I suppose I missed the boat on that. Which is a relief, since the only Russian I really know is food names and the first four words to a dirty joke about goats.

I know I talk about the ungodly amounts of glitter that get thrown around at these things a lot. The truth is that it's really not that much- only that any amount of glitter where glitter oughtn't be is too much glitter. Generally, a 'fistful' of glitter thrown by anyone under the age of ten is going to amount to less than an ounce.

People were putting the entire canister of glitter into the ornaments so that when it moves around it *sparkles!*

Would you like to know what else they didn't cover during the segment on GMA?

The two-part ornaments that we were using don't always close properly. You move them just slightly and the entire contents pour out into the ether.

We all did figure this out eventually.

Unfortunately, we all seemed to figure this out… at the same time. And in the same manner.

So the 8-oz Discoteca in a plastic ball exhaled themselves ceremoniously into the air any time we tried to move them, resulting in some very pissed off parents.

And *She* echoed distantly in my head:

The glitter... is endless.
... endless...

The word bounced around my cranium like a piece of rubber, zig-zagging upward, my heart sinking deeper in my chest as I come to realize that this is all in accordance to the prophecy. *Her* voice was interrupted only by the subtle crunching of my jaw as I clenched my teeth.

Endless.

And the kids, of course, think that's hilarious.
Oh- haha. Great. Funny. Yes.
"Aren't we going to paint the outside of these? Like they did on the TV?"

I froze. I was absolutely incapable of coming up with a solution to this. All the other materials were in the closet and if I brought them out it was sure to create another level of chaos to this that I was wholly not prepared to immerse myself in.

I just... I was just...

I was inhaling glitter. There were pounds of the stuff on the floors, trying to walk was a slippage hazard because the amount of glitter on the floor made it feel like an ice skating rink, literally ALL of the glitter that I had set out was no longer in any kind of container and instead roamed wild amongst its brethren and you....

.... you want me to add PAINT?

Oh. Oh my gods. HA! Ha... ooooooh...

"Sorry, that wasn't something that we prepared for."

Stay mad about it.

As these things tend to go, the chaos ended around the one-hour mark. We were empty with about half an hour to go and I started cleaning up. I was out at three. This was enough time to get to the Urgent Care before it closed so I could at least figure out why it feels like someone socked me in the jaw.

The nurse asked me why I was covered in glitter. I told her where I worked. She said I was 'lucky.'

My heart hurts for you, lady.

So it turns that I have TMJ syndrome, which is just a recurring joint pain. Awesome. How do I fix it?

Page two, section one- bullet point one:
Reducing Stress.

....endless...

We came upon the one-year anniversary of the Glue Famine on my birthday. Well... that is to say that we came upon a perceived one-year anniversary on my birthday. There really is no way of telling when glue became a hot commodity in retrospect. You never really notice how much you need something until it's gone.

I would have liked to say that the surplus of glue has been holding steady for this entire time, but on this date I was brought to the attention of the yet-again-yawning void of the glue section. There was still some on the drive aisle, and I do stipulate: some. I suspected that much of it would be gone in the course of the week.

That's right- slime was popular again; Gods help us.

But I tried to look on the bright side- it was just not my problem anymore.

With my workload quadrupled just in time for the Christmas season, I had problems enough to spare. But I could already tell that it was no picnic at the front end of the store by the constant questions over the radio. About 75% of the staff are brand spankin' new to the store and had no idea where anything was.

On December 2nd, we had (yet another) slime event. I have come to expect at least one a month. However, instead of it being a free event, it was part of our Saturday morning kid's craft class- which costs $2 a head. I did not teach this class, as I was busy building a throne out of cardboard boxes in the back room so that I may lord over my crew of hard-working assistants during this hectic time of year.

Oh, just kidding. You all know I'm the only one back there, processing five times my workload while the management gets huffy over me working overtime because the crew that I was supposed to have all quit.

However, the class was handed off to one of our new employees. I only walked by once, but she seemed ultimately perplexed by the ordeal. I locked eyes with her on my way to the office and it appeared as though she were signaling telepathically: 'help me.'

Ah, but I had work to do.

The two-dollar-fee deterred some people, but not all people. We have gentrified the slime. We have taken this low-cost, low-effort activity and charged a fee for it, making it inaccessible to all but the most elite of slime-lovers. Will our greed never cease?

Are you kidding? This is America. I'm sure there's more.

But in any case, the drama of this event supplied itself in the form of a conversation over the headset.

"A woman wants to know if there's any latex in the slime." This is a reasonable request, as latex allergies can be some of the most severe.

"No, there is no latex in the slime."
Pause.
"She would like to know what the slime is made of."

"Glue, baking soda, contact lens solution."
Pause.
"She would like to know if it is made with borax."

Borax allergies are kind of rare and the chemical itself is used in hypoallergenic detergents. But during the height of the Slime Fad during the spring, there was an article circulating about a little girl in Iowa who got chemical burns from handling slime without gloves.

The science was legitimate and the concerns were real- but to get serious chemical burns you would have to be exposed to it pretty much 24/7 for two weeks, which is what happened with that little girl.

Nonetheless, people encountered the 'Little Girl Gets Chemical Burns from Homemade Slime' headline and we've already discussed the general public's reading comprehension. And people were chomping at the bit to find reasons to ban this Weird Thing The Youth Are Doing.

So it was by legal decree from a number of parents that Slime was hereby Outlawed.

That lasted an entire week, just like the slime ban at schools lasted a week. I've discovered that most things last a week. Weeks last about a week. Sometimes.

But the article makes the rounds again every once in awhile, and there are certain parents... well...

... having taught the kids classes every Saturday morning for half a year...

"Tell Mrs Cleary that the amount of borax in the contact lens solution is small enough that Ashley should should be fine."

However, my response was cut off in the middle by someone else saying 'yes' and another saying 'no,'- and our radios are only capable of handling one input at a time. So what the new girl heard was:

"Tell Mrs Cleary that ▓▓▓▓▓▓▓▓▓▓▓▓▓▓▓▓ be fine."

But, see, no one ever knows when someone

else is talking, so we all just assumed that she got our answer. Until-

"She wants to know all the ingredients." I could hear Ashley wailing in the background.

I can't move from the back room. It is, at this point, not an option. Any time spent not packing things into boxes is time wasted.

"All the ingredients are in the red bag in the closet. She's welcome to read the ingredients if she's brought her reading glasses."

This was an acceptable answer, or at least I assumed so because she was silent for the next three hours.

Now, as is the case with most Saturday programming, our classroom schedule was packed. There was an hour in between the kid's class and the afternoon event, which was gingerbread house decorating.

Evidently, a couple people got a little confused and were surprised to find that there was no slime event in the usual time slot.

They were upset. I mean, who wouldn't be upset to find that their gross slime hobby had been replaced by delicious gingerbread? Clearly no one would want to spend an afternoon making a mess out of frosting and baked goods when they could be playing with mildly caustic chemicals and adhesives!

So of course they were upset.

Because that would be absurd.

Now to think that my involvement in the slime shenanigans was hands-off now that my business was cardboard boxes and heavy lifting would also be absurd. After a certain amount of time in the holiday season, the shelves begin to look as though the Grinch has come through and they only get more barren as we move deeper into the cold, cold winter. Things that had been on the shelves for months and months dwindled down to the barest of stock, and it was only December fifth.

People were, of course, pissed. We were out of trees, most toys, fake snow, and the majority of our ornaments. Which meant that all that was left were the things that people didn't really want.

Oh, but someone wanted them. And it was my job to find the things that people wanted.

There are generally three reasons why a person would refuse buying an item in store:

-They fundamentally have no interest in the item

-They have an interest in the item, but have personal reasons for not buying it.

-There is something wrong with the packaging.

No matter how superficial the damage to packaging might be, people will refuse to buy it and therefore it will sit on a shelf for all eternity (if eternity were a much more limited span of time- in this case about nine months.)

But the people ordering gifts from The Internet had no way of knowing this. All they knew was that we had it.

A bracelet-weaving kit was positively ruined by a handful of slime that had been left on the shelf above it and not cleaned up in time. Completely covered in blue-and-pink glitter glue, absolutely dried and stuck to the box. Trying to pry it up from the packaging ripped a hole, making it unworthy of shipping.

In the Beanie Babies (yes, they still make those) I found two penguins stuck to each other via a flourescent orange substance that had bonded the fibers of their bellies together in a way that looked, honestly, a little obscene.

And in the colored pencils- you guessed it: the Tiny Bison suspended in a hardened glob. Now, whether this was the same tiny bison or a different tiny bison remains to be determined as no one on staff knows how to identify one bison from another. Our in-house biologist only works summers.

But of course this wasn't done. Not when there's money to be made! So mid-month, we had another Slime Sunday! Where you could bring your child to the store to make a 'melted snowman' out of slime while you shop for Christmas presents without them seeing.

Now, once again, I was not there for this one because the mountain of orders piling high behind me just kept getting bigger. But I did see them preparing for the event as I was gathering toys like the over-worked elf that I apparently am.

Understand, of course, that the holidays hit us hard and that there really aren't that many bottles of clear glue left at this point. And clear is, as I have mentioned, one of the most popular variations of slime- to that point that slime primadonnas will refuse to work with its inferior opaque predecessor.

So it was decided that we would use the last of our clear glue and then stretch the recipe by mixing it with white so that we could keep up with the ever-rotating crowd of five-year olds.

I need to stress that this was not my plan.

Because the theme was 'snowman,' there was no intention to use colorants.

This was not my idea.

Which means that the children were playing around with semi-translucent white gelatinous material.

Not my idea, not my idea, not my idea.

It looked like… um..

Well…

Um...

UM...

You see, when a mommy slime and a daddy slime love each other very much...

I had no hand in this. I was in the back trying to fit things in boxes and mentally composing a professional-yet-stern letter to our state representatives about why I deserve to live. I was in no way responsible for distributing quantities of a substance somewhat resembling an inappropriate bodily fluid.

For reasons that seem obvious, this was never mentioned again.

Now, the rest of the season went as most seasons go, but for those who have not been initiated into Christmas Hell, I shall supply you with yet another bulleted list.

-During the three weeks that my workload was inhumane, my knee dislocated while packing a large shipment of frames. I screamed and no one heard me. Eventually, I just popped my knee back in place and vowed to buy better shoes.

-During this nonsense, the one person that we'd hired to help me quit in the middle of his second shift. I was told that we're just going to have to 'suffer through it.' I told the new boss that I was the 'Queen of Suffering.'

-The Christmas music didn't start playing until December 17th. I was taking bets on how long they would go without noticing. Unfortunately, this bet was with myself because if I mentioned it to anyone I would have surely lost.

-The Christmas CD includes at least three ads where *She* talks about slime as a Christmas gift. I know, of course, that *She's* talking about ingredients for slime but I just kind of imagine someone sticking an entire glob of slime straight into a stocking.

-The CD also includes about 20% more "Jesus is the Reason for the Season" variety of songs, which is not only factually incorrect but also kind of rude to the devil worshipers that work at the shipping dock.

-People were super salty over the fact that we had a single drive aisle specifically for Hannukkah. On more than one occasion, customers would point it out to me because we had this but not a section specifically for Christmas card-making. (Which we did.)

-See, you can't just straight-up say that you're offended by the reminder that people of other cultures exist in the same parking lot as you- like you can't say 'I really don't like that you acknowledge that Jewish people live here.'

-You have to point out the blatant injustice of being diminished by the presence of non-Christians in this community. You have to say 'why do THEY get a section and we only get AN ENTIRE ONE HALF OF THE STORE!?'

-Insert a gif of Dudley Dursley here.

-The figurine of Baby White Jesus was stolen from our display Nativity set on December 5th, which was three days earlier than last year.

-Our Spring decor arrived on December 7th and oh- people were not pleased as the floral section popped with bright forsythias. "It's December," they cried as they gestured to the sunny yellows and new greens of spring. "Oh, but ma'am- you were asking for pointsettias clear in the month of August." These are things you wish to say to them, but at the risk of losing your job- so it is acceptable to simply nod and say 'what a shame.'

-After three years of working at this place, the District Manager finally spoke to me to congratulate me on all the money that I had made the company over the course of the past two weeks.

-He ended this conversation by handing me the coveted Golden Scratch-Off Ticket.

-You see, instead of raises or anything actually useful, our company deemed it a totally-not-tone-deaf incentive to hand all the underpaid employees a scratch off ticket in recognition for their exemplary work. The scratch-off ticket will give you a chance to win wonderful prizes, such as- an extra 15-minute break, snack food, a parking space next to the building, and so on.

-It should be noted that our store is the middle building in a strip mall and that there is no parking spot next to our building. Unless you want to aggravate traffic.

-Ah, but he gave me a GOLD ticket, which only the DM is capable of giving out. What prizes and treasure may be concealed in this piece of card stock? A gift card to the company website- where I can buy t-shirts with the company logo on them!

-The redemption code, of course, did not work. It was the thought that counts, I suppose.

-Soon after, my hours were reduced to two-hour shifts, which is just enough of a paycheck for me to be filled with hatred.

-By the last week before Christmas, the Slime Drive Aisle was reduced to only one panel, harnessing the power of only about a dozen bottles of glue. I walked past a group of mothers discussing how they simply did not understand it, simply didn't understand it, simply didn't understand it. Oh- but their nieces had entire LABS in the basement dedicated to this.

-The life-size Santa figurine was broken off of his baseboard and moved to the back. For the next three weeks, the crew moved him closer and closer to my desk- always facing me.

-In the final week, he was put on clearance and displayed with the Christmas trees, where he could see me from the register.

-He was purchased, promptly.

However, he sat in the classroom for a day while the buyer got a big enough car to haul him away. When he came to pick Kringle up, I was the only person available. I escorted him from the store by way of wheeled dolly, but to get him into the man's SUV I had to pick St Nick up by the crotch.

-I'm on the naughty list for the next three lifetimes.

-Christmas Eve was marked by a sudden interest in last minute Hatchimals, which we'd been out of for about a month- but everyone seemed to think that we'd have the most asked-for toy of the last two years just laying around. And oh-they weren't happy.

-I have ruined Christmas four times this year, which comes second place only to 2011.

-Now the story there is that I was working in a call center focusing around professional photography. I worked in the Preschool department, meaning that these were 'baby's first pictures.' Pressure was high. During a training session, our instructor took a call from the floor to show us how easy it was.

-To make a long story short, the call actually took about forty-five minutes because a self-described 'very beige person' accidentally ordered her son's photos to be an 'obnoxious bright blue' instead of slate grey and now 'the entire decor is thrown off' and- here it comes: 'these were going to be Christmas presents. You RUINED CHRISTMAS.'

-This is when I began counting the instances wherein I ruin Christmas.

-I worked at that call center for exactly one week before the multiple order interfaces, piling paperwork, and unholy screeching of repressed housewives became too much for me and I had to quit. And in that week, I ruined Christmas a total of six times. Bonus points for the woman who asked for my full name so she could report me, specifically, to the Better Business Bureau so that I would be blacklisted from ever working ever again in these here United States.
-You can see how well that worked out.
-Slime kits accounted for roughly 10% of my orders this season.
-"All I want for Christmas is GLUE"
-"It's the most wonderful SLIME of the year."
-"I'll have a Glue Christmas without you.

Christmas Eve is a very odd time of the year. There is no telling what kind of a crowd will be brought in, so they do their best to prepare for anything.

In hindsight, perhaps staffing the store with seven cashiers was a bit of overkill, given that for about a solid hour, we didn't see a single customer enter the store. The customers we did see were either buying small amounts of things or returning things they'd bought (and used) previously.

However, it is of note that each time I passed the glue display, there would be less and less bottles there. And by the time I made it to the end of my shift at noon, there was none left.

People really do listen to *Her*.

But if there is one lesson to be learned from the frenzy brought on by the Christmas season, it is this:

It ends.

If you blink at the right time, one second it's Christmas and the next it isn't. The music returns to

Top 40, and all that's left is a trail of glitter and the faint smell of cinnamon. The world returns a regular kind of chaos, and we emerge from this stronger than we entered.

One would hope, in a literary setting, that a story like this can only culminate in a dramatic climax. However, there is a poetic conclusion to be had in the acceptance of a new normal. And as we come upon the one-year anniversary of this journal, I find it an appropriate time for closure.

Oh, slime is still a thing here. Let's not mince words- come January, we were still having one slime event a month. We still had the slime drive aisle, but it amounted to about one panel on the back end of a 'science project' display where that kind of thing *fucking belongs.* This was displayed, discreetly, in a portion of the store that people rarely visit.

It seemed, honestly, as though we were hiding it. As though we were luring it back into the glue caverns from whence it came, preparing to seal it for all of eternity. Instead of glue, our guests were greeted with the calming display of miniature electric water fountains and lush plastic greenery. We will call this our... denial phase. Cover up the wound until we can find our time to heal.

Don't knock it- denial serves a purpose in the healing process.

But any fan of the adventure genre (and this certainly was an adventure) will tell you that the narrative must be left open for a sequel.

And oh- we had that.

Now, when Christmas ends, that is a common time to take care of neglected inventory. The week after New Years, customers passed us in shifting shadows- hurrying through the wind and snow and hastily purchasing their googly eyes before disappearing into a world of white. The store fell into a hush. We were dormant, like seeds.

Or bears. You know- I think bears works better in this metaphor.

But about that sequel.

The post-Christmas sales valley was a perfect time to take a look at our inventory and see what might have gone missing during the holiday. It is important to note that not all instances of incorrect quantity are the result of outright theft. Sometimes things get misscanned or damaged and not taken out of inventory. Some things are lost behind shelves of things no one wants. It is important that we not take every instance of missing merchandise as a case of theft.

No one is quite certain how or when it happened; whether it was all at once or over the course of the entire season. But what we do know is that we were surprised to find that at some point between November and January, one-hundred and seventy-two bottles of glue disappeared from our shelves.

And as the Sticky-Finger Bandit vanished into the snow, I discovered…

… that it was no longer my problem.

The moral of this story, if we were to boil one from it, I suppose is this- there's a lot that can happen in the span of a year and we are nothing if not resilient. Things change, but so do people. And sometimes you just gotta pop your jaw back into place, put on a pair of rubber gloves, and listen to the children babble for a few hours.

    This, too, shall pass.

    And if it doesn't pass, you find a way to accept it.

    Eventually it all became no longer my problem- and I no longer cared.

    And as a parting gift, here are some photos of the stray cats living behind my dumpster, as promised.

The Very End

Find other stories by Lee Bradford at thecannibalcoalition.com!

Good, Clean Dirt
"His great aunt twice removed would be rolling around in her grave if she weren't freshly dead and also completely fictional." Why is small-time crook Reuben Weller following around a florist in a remote mountain town? For the money, of course! But things get weird when he stumbles, quite literally onto a very big secret. Watch out for those mountain-dwelling hipsters: they believed in the old gods before it was cool.

A Simple Spell and the Dangers of Online Dating
You'd think you'd know a guy after dating him for a few months- Sheesh.

One day you're cuddling under the blankets, the next you're running from him in the woods because you traded human bones for necromancy after feeding him a cursed muffin.

Dating sure isn't what it used to be.

All this and more at your local Internet.
There's more to life than glue.
But, arguably, not much more.

Made in the USA
Columbia, SC
16 April 2018